Text Copyright © 2025 by Paul Washington

Photo Credits: The Washington Family; Tanya Rawlins -The Photo Firm

All rights reserved. No part of this publication may be reproduced, distributed, or transmitted in any form or by any means, including photocopying, recording, or other electronic or mechanical methods without the prior written permission of the publisher.

Printed in the United States of America

Name: Paul Washington, Author

Title: The Frontline Hero: A Story of Bravery, Wisdom, Kindness and Love

Summary: Engaging stories of a U.S. Army Veteran serving on the frontline of the Vietnam War enduring unimaginable challenges but finds strength through his faith, love and kindness.

Identifiers:
ISBN: 978-1-956292-38-1 (hardcover)
ISBN: 978-1-956292-39-8 (paperback)

Subject: God's Love | Childhood Trauma | Family Support | Service and Sacrifice

Book Cover Design © 2025 by SUSU Entertainment LLC

THE FRONTLINE HERO

A STORY OF BRAVERY, WISDOM, KINDNESS AND LOVE

PAUL WASHINGTON

INTRODUCTION

This book aims to delve into the personal life and multifaceted experiences of a Vietnam Veteran, Mr. Paul Washington, who fought through the tumultuous period on the frontline of the Vietnam War, illuminating not just the battles fought on distant fields, but the battles that raged within the hearts and minds of the soldiers, civilians, and their families.

Mr. Washington contributes his survival to God's protection and is very transparent in always giving him the glory, honor and praise. By giving voice to those who experienced the war firsthand—veterans, activists, and survivors, this American history will uncover the enduring legacy of Vietnam, a conflict that reshaped nations and altered lives forever. Follow Mr. Washington's journey from childhood to adulthood to understand not just what happened, but why it matters, as we seek to honor the stories that continue to resonate in our collective memory.

Contents

CHAPTER 1
    THE KID FROM KEMP STREET 6

CHAPTER 2
    FREE TO BE ME.. 9

CHAPTER 3
    TEACHER'S HELPER 12

CHAPTER 4
    THE ENTREPRENEUR 15

CHAPTER 5
    WHO SAID THAT I AM POOR? 17

CHAPTER 6
    LIVING OFF OF THE LAND 20

CHAPTER 7
    PAIN, ABUSE, AND TRAUMA 23

CHAPTER 8
    THE SHOE SHINE BOY..27

CHAPTER 9
    TRUE STORIES FROM THE ELDERS 30

CHAPTER 10
    PETER AND HIS RED BICYCLE 35

CHAPTER 11
    HIGH SCHOOL INTERGRATION...38

CHAPTER 12
    MR. POPULARITY 41

CHAPTER 13
    HIGH SCHOOL SWEETHEART 43

CHAPTER 14
    DRAFTED TO THE VIETNAM WAR 45

CHAPTER 15
    WHAT HAPPENED TO THE AMERICAN DREAM? 54

CHAPTER 16
    HELP OUR VETERANS 61

CHAPTER 17
    DO'S AND DON'TS TO ASK A VETERAN 67

CHAPTER 18
    FINDING THE LOVE OF MY LIFE 71

CHAPTER 19
    FAMILY IS EVERYTHING 75

CHAPTER 20
    WISE WORDS FROM A VIETNAM VETERAN 78

ACKNOWLEDGMENTS 84

LETTER TO MY DADDY 86

LETTER FROM FORMER PRESIDENT BARACK OBAMA ... 88

YELLOW ROSE 89

IN MEMORY OF 90

ABOUT THE AUTHOR 91

PHOTO COLLAGE 93

BOOKS OF THE BIBLE 124

CHAPTER 1

THE KID FROM KEMP STREET

Life was good for Peter. He was a very fun-loving, active, kind and inquisitive child. Peter was the third oldest of his parent's nine children, seven boys and two girls. He was born Paul Michael Washington in 1949, but was called Peter by a lady in the neighborhood. He didn't know it until later in life, but his mom wasn't fond of the name Peter, however, it stuck with him throughout his early childhood. Peter grew up on 5727 Kemp Street, the Lunnon Addition area on the east side of Houston, Texas. His dad was a filling station attendant, and later became a truck driver, and his mom was a housekeeper and cook in the cafeteria.

For years, Peter's parents rented a room in a house in the Third Ward area of Houston but later was happy to find a house, somewhere they could call home in the east end on Kemp Street, paying $13.60 per month for rent. Only Peter, his mom and dad and four brothers lived on Kemp Street, his other four siblings weren't born yet. Although a two-bedroom, one bathroom home was small for a family of 7, it seemed big enough for their family, and they made it work. Peter's mom always wanted a new house with more bedrooms, but it never happened, which motivated Peter to work hard because he knew the struggle that he saw his parents go through, so he wanted better.

Peter and his siblings weren't strangers to hard work. Every Saturday morning their mom would yell, "Rise and shine!" They knew that Saturdays was cleaning day. Sometimes if they were too slow getting up, she would threaten them and they got up with the quickness. Every sibling had their own responsibilities, like, washing dishes, washing clothes, hanging the clothes on the clothes line and folding clothes. Peter's duties were to clean the bathroom and mop the floors.

Peter loved to play outdoors with his siblings and neighborhood friends. Some of their games didn't have a name, however, all they knew was that they were fun to play. Most of their games were unique because they were created by Peter and his siblings. Games like, pushing a tire down the street to see who could roll it the fastest, playing marbles and jacks, and walking on stilts that they made out of 2, 2x4 blocks of wood with supports for their feet, enabling them to walk a high distance above the ground. The entire neighborhood was owned by a black man named Mike Lunnon. Mike was loved by the entire community. He had a friend named Rufus; a white man who helped him purchase the land. Some of the white folk in the city would say, "Look at nigger-loving Rufus." They didn't like that he had helped a black man buy land.

For many years Mike Lunnon owned acres of land in the community. Everyone including Peter felt happy to know that the land they lived on was owned by a black man. The white folks hated that he owned so much land, so one day they pretended to be his friends and took him to a bar getting him good and liquored up. While intoxicated they asked him to sign a few papers. Mike didn't know what he was signing and wasn't in his right mind but agreed. The next day when he had sobered up, he was furious to find out that he had signed the land over to a white guy and his family. This devastated Peter and the entire black community. Black families use to own many acres of land, but because of their lack of knowledge and the conniving ways of white people a lot of their assets were stolen from them.

Like many in the community, Peter and his family experienced a multitude of hardships. His dad was in and out of his life throughout his childhood. One day his dad was cleaning his rifle, cocked it, and mistakenly shot himself in the leg. This caused a major shift in their family. Peter's dad wasn't able to work and was put on disability. It was a financial strain for the family so they decided that their boys would relocate to Crockett, Texas and live with their aunts and uncles for a better living. Marvin, the oldest, moved in with Uncle Buck, Donald settled in with Uncle Jim O. and Aunt Lizzie, Uncle Ben and Aunt Willie took in Peter and Leon stayed with Aunt Mattie and Uncle Tim. Carl moved in with Aunt Cardia, his dad's sister. He was the furthest away because later they moved to West Texas and it was years before the brothers saw him again. The beauty of family was they helped out where it was needed and the boys were grateful.

CHAPTER 2

FREE TO BE ME

Peter fell in love with Crockett, Texas because it was true country living. His Aunt Willie had all the fruit trees imaginable. There were fig trees, apple trees, plum trees, pear trees, peach trees, and pecan trees. Peter absolutely loved fruit, he even enjoyed picking the berries from the vines. Peter felt like he was living in paradise. When it was time to eat, Aunt Willie would yell, "Peter! Peter! Time to eat!" Aunt Willie was an awesome cook. She made everything from scratch. Peter's favorite was her moist and buttery homemade biscuits that would melt in your mouth. He loved to pick fruit from the fruit trees because she would use the fruits to make preserves, jellies and jams to spread on the biscuits.

Peter felt free as a bird in Crockett because he roamed their acres of land as he pleased. There was so much space, he didn't feel cramped like he did in the city. He enjoyed the hustle and bustle of city life, but some may feel that there is a benefit to country living, like unstructured playtime, less stress, sharper cognitive skills, and overall happiness. It may seem like a small thing but Peter enjoyed the little pleasures like gazing into the clear night's sky to see the beauty of the stars.

His Uncle Ben was a very talented man, building their church from the ground up. Peter felt like a growing young man as he helped his uncle build the church, by handing him the tools that he needed. Peter loved to roam around in the woods and was never afraid of snakes. He admired the talents and strength of his uncle. He would watch him shoot a squirrel, even a bird off a telephone pole with his rifle. Uncle Ben was a jack of all trades and Peter learned a lot from him, like how to be self-sufficient, hard-working, and the responsibility of being a wonderful and loving husband and father.

Uncle Ben was a man of good character, a great provider and protector for the family. Peter loved his family and was happy to spend his first Christmas in Crockett, Texas. Christmas morning his uncle woke him up and told him that Santa Claus had left him something. Peter was delighted and felt so special racing out of the bed to see what he had. To Peter's surprise, Uncle Ben told him to look on the top shelf.

Peter pulled out a bag of cookies, the right side was vanilla and the left side was chocolate. "Is this for me? Is it really all mine?" Peter excitedly asked. Uncle Ben responded. "Yes, Peter! It is all yours." You see, Peter was a very happy and humbled child, the smallest gesture of kindness made Peter smile. No matter how big or small the gift, Peter was grateful to have a pack of cookies to himself. Peter remembered how his Aunt Willie would never throw anything away. If you had holes in your clothes, she would find some material and patch it up, even if it didn't match.

Everyone wore hammy downs. Peter only had two pair of shoes that were only worn for school and church. He had one pair of boots that he mistakenly walked on the side of. His aunt would scold him for wearing out the side of his boots. Sometimes he was afraid to walk because he didn't know if he was walking correctly. When the children were at home, everyone walked around barefooted. You would get popped by the adults if you were caught wearing your good shoes, school clothes or church clothes around the house. This was the way it was in the community and everybody knew the rules.

Peter had the same group of neighborhood friends that he went to school and church with. He grew up with a whole community of believers, this is why Peter loves to go to church today. You would get chastised from the neighbors if you were doing wrong and no one would get mad. Adults supported one another when it came to raising their kids. Children didn't talk back to their elders or they would get slapped in the mouth. You may not have agreed with your parents' rules but you obeyed and respected their decisions.

Children stayed in a child's place. You were seen but never heard, they didn't get in grown folk conversations. It was fun being a kid, because your only responsibilities were to do your chores, respect and obey your elders, go to church, play with your friends and do well in school. Peter was a good child but he understood that if he misbehaved in any way there would be consequences of his actions, this is how you learn right from wrong. Elders took control and always had the final say so.

CHAPTER 3

TEACHER'S HELPER

Peter enjoyed going to elementary school. He was liked by his peers and teachers. Peter was excited when one of his teachers gave him the task of ringing the school bell in the classroom, a handheld bell at the beginning of the day. He enjoyed being a teacher's helper because he could write very neatly and was often asked by his teacher to write notes on the chalkboard. Peter enjoyed recess because he was very athletic. He could run fast and loved playing football. Peter was smart in school but didn't like math because he didn't understand it, and having 37-38 students in one class, there was no one-on-one time with the teacher or tutoring after school. Peter had a cheerful spirit; he was popular, with many friends, especially the girls. He always stood out because of his kindness, positivity and charming behavior.

At home, Peter was his uncle's right-hand man. He watched his Uncle Ben kill hogs, chickens, and cows. Afterwards, everyone in the neighborhood would eat good. It was so much fun to see the whole community coming together. Uncle Ben had a mule tied by a rope and it would walk around in circles pumping the juice out of the sugar cane that went in a vacuum to make the syrup. It would make the thickest, tastiest and sweetest syrup that was shared by the entire community. Aunt Willie would tend to the garden where they grew tomatoes, collard greens, squash, yams, okra, and peppers.

Families in the community never went hungry because they were raised on homegrown food. It was good food without the artificial preservatives that is often included in today's food. Uncle Ben and Aunt Willie rarely went to town, but when they had to go, Peter loved to tag along. Uncle Ben would let him ride and they would go and buy a few items that they couldn't grow. One day the two of them drove to town and when they came out of the store, Uncle Ben couldn't find their car. Back in the 1950's everyone seemed to drive black cars with the same make and model and all of the cars were parked the same way. It wasn't until hours later that they found their car in the parking lot.

At school there was no food program, Peter took his lunch in a syrup bucket. His Aunt Willie would make him peanut butter sandwiches or preserve sandwiches. The wives would fix their husband's lunches in gallon buckets with food off the land. The community was predominately black and everyone looked out for each other. It was the Jones family, Washington family, and Smith family that lived on the same block. Peter and his brothers were 11 months apart. They all lived in Crockett with their families and loved to spend time together. It was like a family reunion when they would come over with his aunts and uncles.

Where the boys lived it was so much land, they were able to play football, racing games, even built a go cart by hand with a lawn mower engine that they would take turns driving. Besides Christmas, Easter was another favorite holiday for Peter. They helped their Aunt Willie pick berries to color the eggs. They didn't use easter egg coloring, they had a bucket and would mash the berries until it was filled with the juice and used that juice from the berries to paint their easter eggs.

As a parent or guardian, you should do everything in your power to give your children a good life. Provide them with a safe and comfortable environment, teach them about God, respect and love for oneself and others. As the adult, you must ensure that they are getting a good education, providing healthy meals, clothing, and opportunities for them to enjoy life and have fun.

While meeting the physical needs is important and a family priority, spending quality time with your children may be one of the most important critical things that can help a child's emotional development and growth. When you spend quality time together it allows you to teach and your child to learn, which will strengthen your relationship. By being around their parent, it helps boosts your child's self-esteem and self-image. Enjoy your life with your children. You will become closer and have a more loving and nurturing bond.

CHAPTER 4

THE ENTREPRENEUR

Peter had a multitude of jobs. His aunt and uncle bought him a wagon to occasionally haul wood. He was also responsible for cleaning the bathrooms, mow, edge and hoe four to five front and back yards of white people in the area. Peter was a very responsible child and an extremely hard worker; he knew how to hustle to earn a dollar. He never had any problems collecting his money from the white people, but he was disturbed because back then black people were only allowed to go to the back door of a white person's home, unless they were washing windows or cutting their grass in the front yard. Peter walked to the back door and was thankful to be paid on time, even getting a few extra dollars.

Peter was so happy to earn his own money. His first purchase was putting a brand-new suit on layaway for $14.00. As a teenager, he was a feed store worker, and a dish washer for many of his neighbors. Years later he worked two jobs as a welder's assistant, and a sand blaster at a steel mill manufacturing company. He had worked very hard over the years and saved a lot of money. Peter confided in one of his elder neighbors back home and left the money with her to save for him. He wholeheartedly trusted her and wanted to save up his money for school clothes and school supplies. Peter was working more hours than his mother and father combined. He was glad that all of the hours he had worked and the money he had saved, he didn't have to go without, he could pay for everything he needed for himself.

Living in the country was a breath of fresh air for Peter. He made a lot of friends but was saddened when he had to relocate back home with his mom in Houston. The school requested his birth certificate and other documents that his aunt didn't have available. Peter was thankful for everything he was taught by his aunt and uncle. They exposed him to a different way of living which shaped him into the man he is today.

CHAPTER 5

WHO SAID THAT I AM POOR?

Peter reminisced when he was seven-years-old and returned back home to Houston to visit. The neighbors would ask, "Mollie, who is that little boy?" Mollie was Peter's biological Mother. She would answer. "That's my son, Peter." Peter wore overalls with patches of different fabrics. He looked like one of the Beverly Hillbillies. Peter didn't know that he was poor, "Who said that I am poor?" He thought. Peter's family was truly poor, but being rich or poor is a state of mind. You are only poor when you admit defeat. Having a mindset of being poor is an easy out, it means you don't believe in yourself, have evil thoughts and feel that others owe you something. Poor, is the decision to give up financially. Jesus said, "The poor will always be around **Matthew 26:11**, but it is up to you whether or not you decide to be one of them." This never crossed Peter's mind because he was happy and carefree and loved himself and his family.

Peter remembered when he was younger, him and his little brother Leon would walk half-way to school before they would get sent back home. They were left at home because they weren't old enough to attend school. His mom and dad were working and the rest of the siblings were at school. Peter's parents never left food for them to eat and his brother knew that they would be hungry, so he climbed up to the top shelf and grabbed a box of cereal. Him and Peter ate the whole box of cereal in one sitting. Both of the boys were scorned by their parents when they got home.

One day Peter and Donald, his older brother walked to the store and Donald bought a pack of cigarettes. Back then, convenient store owners were allowed to sell anything to anyone, and it wasn't against the law to sell cigarettes to children. His brother Donald puffed on the cigarette and passed it to Peter. Peter puffed on it for the first time at age 6, never inhaling. They stopped at the store and bought some fruit, this was Peter's ultimate favorite, he loved fruit. He ate a banana and it tasted nothing like a banana, he couldn't taste anything but that strong taste of the tobacco from the cigarette. Peter was upset because he thought the cigarette had taken his taste buds away. That day was his start and stop of smoking at age 6. He never touched a cigarette again in his life.

Peter and his brothers had many chores. His family had a bucket that they used at night when they had to go to the bathroom. Peter was responsible for emptying it out the next morning to eliminate the odors. They would take gallon pee buckets, put the buckets under each bed, and in the morning, pour it out, sit it out in the sun to get the pee smell out. Some may refer to them as chamber pots. It wasn't his favorite job to do, but it had to be done.

Growing up, Peter didn't have many issues with discrimination during childhood, but remembered one Saturday while shopping at Woolworths in downtown Houston with his mom he had gotten thirsty and ran up to the water fountain and was immediately grabbed by his mom. She said, "Peter, you can't drink out of that fountain, this one over here is for us." Like most curious seven-year old's, Peter asked, "Why?" Mom added, "The sign says, White Only." "We have to drink out of this one, it says, Colored Only." "Does the water taste different?" Peter asked. Mom chuckled. "No, Peter it doesn't taste different. It is the rules that we have to follow for now." Peter's mom showed him the signs on the restroom doors; it was the same as the water fountains, "White Only" and "Colored Only." Peter felt that it didn't make sense and was a stupid rule. After shopping, Peter started to get hungry.

The store had two levels with a restaurant attached. They allowed black and white customers to shop together but not eat together. Black customers could only eat downstairs while the white customers would dine upstairs. Peter knew in his heart that black customers should be treated the same as the white customers because all money is green. "Why should the color of your skin matter in the service you receive?" He thought. Peter was confident and knew in his heart that one day a change was going to come because we were all wonderfully and fearfully made by God.

CHAPTER 6

LIVING OFF OF THE LAND

Peter's play Grandma, "Baby" asked Peter's mother Mollie if he could go live with her niece Lillie Brown, a school teacher in Smithfield, Texas; this was after returning back from Crockett. Lillie's children were grown and her and her husband needed someone to help take care of chores on the farm. Peter was happy when he arrived in Smithfield because Aunt Lillie, as he called her, immediately took him shopping, buying him new clothes, underwear, and shoes, everything that he needed.

He enjoyed being in Smithfield because his aunt would make a variety of cakes, bread pudding, cobblers, sweet potato pies, and his favorite fruit cake. He loved to go to the sausage house with his uncle to get meat to grill; because of him Peter absolutely loves to grill meats today. Peter enjoyed living in Smithfield but when he went to school, his aunt told him that she would no longer refer to him as Peter but Michael, his middle name. He didn't like that his Aunt Lillie attempted to change his name. He liked his birth name.

Most of the food that the family ate came from their land. Peter learned a lot living on a farm with his Aunt Lillie and Uncle Sonny. They introduced Peter to picking cotton and he loved to watch his Uncle Sonny milk the cows. At the time, he was too young to help but enjoyed watching him strain the milk and churn it to get the butter. As a teenager, Peter would get up in the early mornings to put watermelon on the back of his uncle's truck. His uncle backed the truck up to the hog pin so that Peter could feed the hogs watermelon. The watermelons were homegrown by his uncle, and he used them because it was less feed he had to pay for out of his pocket for the hogs. Hogs ate anything, including scraps from the table. Sometimes, he bought feed for the hogs, which was a flour-based mixture but scraps and watermelon was cheaper.

Paul was a fruit lover and didn't like that his uncle wanted him to give the entire watermelon to the hogs. He sneaked and busted the watermelon open and ate as much as he could until his stomach was about to burst, because it was no way in Peter's mind that the hog would eat a brand-new watermelon. Peter would eat the watermelon so fast not to get caught. It is often said jokingly that the black community loves watermelon but many aren't aware that watermelon has a huge health benefit. Watermelon helps with hydration, promotes healthy skin, digestion, and cleanse kidneys. It also helps with hypertension, eye health, provides potassium, asthma prevention, weight control, manages blood sugar, fights inflammation, immune support and more. All jokes aside, eating this sweet and juicy fruit is rich in amino acids, low in calories, decrease your risk of cancers and is very good to you and for you.

Once Peter finished eating his watermelon, he threw the hogs his leftovers. Peter was also trained on killing chickens, this was not his favorite thing to do. He witnessed his aunt grabbing the chicken by the head and going around and around in circles until the chicken's neck was broken. She would drop the chicken on the ground and it hopped around until it fell dead. They immediately put it in hot water to allow the feathers to fall off easier.

After feeding the hogs, it was time to go to the field to pick cotton. Adults used long cotton sacks to pick cotton. Peter had a smaller feed sack converted into a cotton sack with a strap. When Peter was able to pick cotton, he recalled picking cotton with preachers, teachers, entire families all day long in the heat. It was so hot that you could see the sun dancing in the air. To protect yourself from having a heatstroke everyone wore a hat and a long sleeve shirt.

They also picked corn from the corn fields. The men would knock the corn off the stalk to the ground and Peter had to follow the wagon and pick up the corn. This required a lot of physical labor, pulling and bending, which truly wore him out. Peter and the men only did one row at a time, but he noticed one guy would be on his knees in the hot sun all day picking two rows together. This was unheard of for most of the workers but the white folks loved to see this man coming because he worked harder than anyone in the corn field. The sad part is this man probably got paid the same as everyone else but was doing double labor.

CHAPTER 7

PAIN, ABUSE, AND TRAUMA

Peter knew how to find a job. He worked unloading train cars, did custodial work, and delivered newspapers. Nothing was too hard for Peter. Sometimes he got paid more than expected and sometimes less but whatever he made he knew how to save his money. Peter was very close to his neighbor and trusted her to hide his money. One weekend he went home and decided it was time to put some items on layaway in time for school. Peter would buy school clothes for him and his little brother Floyd, they were five years apart. He went to his neighbor's house to collect some of his money and she told him that the money was gone.

Peter fell to his knees asking her what happened to all of his hard-earned money. The neighbor told him that his mom kept questioning her about why Peter would stop by her house so frequently and when I told her, she demanded the money. "I'm sorry Peter, I know that you worked very hard for that money, but your mom came over and took it all," the neighbor explained. Peter stormed out of the house and headed to his parent's house. "Mom where is the money that I saved?" Peter asked. "What money Peter?" Mom asked. As Peter was explaining his mom interrupted and said, "I took all that money, it's gone."

Peter was furious, he stormed out of the house to keep from disrespecting his mom. Peter's mom had suffered a lot of hardships and trauma growing up. Her mom passed away when she was only two-years-old and her dad wasn't able to care for her and her siblings. They were given to a man named Mr. John Taylor; they called him Daddy John. Peter wasn't sure how they were related but was told that Daddy John provided a good living for Peter's mom Mollie and her siblings. Years later, Mollie's grandmother came down and asked for her and her siblings, these were her daughter that had passed away children. As a child, Peter's mom Mollie didn't have a stable place to live for years.

Sadly, a guy she was living with kept messing with her. Mollie was raped repeatedly in her teenage years by this man who lived with her, her grandmother and siblings. After so much drama, Mollie relocated and moved in with her family in Houston. She worked in a restaurant in Houston and was raped again. She was fed up with the constant abuse and got up the nerves to contact the authorities. She told the Houston police officer what had been happening to her for years and was told that he needed to come out to her house for a site visit. When the white, Houston police officer arrived and saw that Mollie was home alone, he raped her too.

This haunted Peter's mom her entire life leaving her to take out her pain on those around her. Mollie endured a lot of pain and constantly released her anger on her children. While working at the restaurant in Houston, Mollie met Jimmy, Peter's dad, they were both from Crockett, Texas. Peter's parents got married shortly after meeting each other because Mollie wanted to escape the abuse. She didn't have anyone to lean on before getting married because a few of her siblings had run away from home and when she finally located her brother he was drafted into the Navy.

Peter's parents had nine children, and in his mind, it was more children than they could afford. Peter and some of his siblings endured abuse from his mom being whooped with a bull whip, switch, extension cord, tree limb, broomstick, all while being naked. Peter's mom didn't stop beating him until she saw his flesh torn and his butt bleeding. If you did anything bad, his dad would call them in the room and you had to place your whole head between his legs and he would hold your head tight with his inner thigh while beating your butt. Peter's dad would say, "You think you're slick but you need one more greasing." His dad, Mr. Jim Floyd Washington was very firm.

Peter was a good child but had some mischievous ways. One day Peter broke in a man's house, stole his watch and wore the watch like it was his own. His dad asked him where he got the watch from, Peter hesitated, but finally admitted that he stole the watch from the man's house. His dad made him return the watch and he was punished by getting a whooping by his dad. He feared being whooped by his dad, but beatings by his mom were torture to Peter and he didn't realize until he was an adult that it was considered child abuse. Peter felt that his mom disliked him. He often wondered if he was adopted because he couldn't believe that his biological mom would be okay torturing her own flesh and blood. Peter was very outgoing and upbeat and felt his mom's sadness and depression made her take her anger out on him.

Peter's mom Mollie beat him badly outside on the side of the house one day that she broke a broom on him and continued to beat him with the broken broom stick until he was bleeding. Peter couldn't count the many black and blue bruises left on his body. He knew that deep down his parents loved him and wanted to provide a good living for their family but because of choices they made and hardships they endured, some of the children had to suffer the consequences. As Peter got older, he shielded away from his mom because of the deep hurt and pain.

CHAPTER 8

THE SHOE SHINE BOY

Peter and his family didn't have much but he didn't know it because he was always a happy, laid-back kid. He had been working hard since he was in the 6th grade, no job was too much for Peter. He worked hard because he liked to have his own money. One day Peter walked in a local barbershop owned by a white man named Mr. Bill Tanner. Peter asked in his southern slang, "Ya'll needs a shine boy?" "Do you know how to shine shoes boy?" Mr. Tanner asked. "Yesssurr, I do!" Peter had never shined a shoe in his life, but he was a quick learner and definitely needed the money.

Peter was happy that Mr. Tanner offered him the job on the spot paying him $8.00 per week to keep the barbershop clean, by sweeping up the hair, cleaning the mirrors, and dusting and shining the customer's shoes. Surprisingly, Peter was given big tips for shining shoes and Mr. Tanner never asked him for one dime of his tip money, always keeping him stocked up with shoe shine polish when it got low. Most of Peter's customers worked at the local brewery and gave him plenty of work, but he didn't mind because he got paid well.

Mr. Tanner drove a white Cadillac and Peter loved to help him keep it clean by sweeping out the inside. Mr. Tanner and his buddies would go golfing, bringing back bags of muddy golf shoes for Peter to clean. This was another one of Peter's hustles, making multiple streams of income. Mr. Tanner was Peter's boss but was like a father figure instilling in Peter how to manage and save his money. Peter earned Mr. Tanner's trust and he started cutting his grass, also referring Peter to do his mother's yard, his sister's yard and washing the family's cars. Before long, Peter was working for the entire family. Peter never charged them an exact dollar amount for his work, but let's just say the entire family was truly generous. Peter tried to save money but it was hard because his parents constantly asked him for money.

One day Peter got frustrated with his parents always asking him for money and shared this with Mr. Tanner. He immediately became furious telling Peter that it wasn't right what they were doing. Mr. Tanner was willing to talk with Peter's parents, but Peter begged him not to mention it to them. One thing you don't do is to tell a man, especially a black man how to raise his kids. Unlike some white men, Mr. Tanner was different. He saw that Peter had a good character, strong work ethic, trustworthy and kind so he was willing to invest in him.

Peter had so many businesses and Mr. Tanner made sure everyone knew it, referring him to his family and friends. Mr. Bill Tanner was very influential in Peter's life. Peter was shocked when Mr. Tanner wrote him a check for $1,000.00 and gave it to him as a gift. He took his time and invested wisdom into Peter on how to make money and create a lifestyle that he could afford while developing a savings strategy to help him work towards having options later in life. No one had ever educated Peter in any money goals. Mr. Tanner told Peter that it wasn't the money that you make but how much you can keep.

Adopting a healthy money mindset involves managing money but also creating a lifestyle that aligns with your financial capabilities and future aspirations. Peter felt like a growing young man listening to Mr. Tanner share his knowledge about financial freedom. Mr. Tanner emphasized the importance of creating short-term and long-term goals, getting a life insurance policy, living within your means, understanding needs versus wants, which is crucial to achieve your financial goals.

He encouraged Peter to one day save for retirement and invest his money. Some of the information he talked to Peter about he didn't quite understand as a teenager but he knew that Mr. Tanner cared about his future. Peter loved Mr. Tanner. He continued to work for him for many years, constantly getting referrals for business. As a child, Peter was never told by his family to hate white people, but just not to trust them. Peter was grateful for Mr. Tanner's friendship and as he became an adult, him and Mr. Tanner remained close friends until he passed away.

CHAPTER 9

TRUE STORIES FROM THE ELDERS

Peter loved listening to the elders share stories. He remembered as a little boy hearing stories from his mom about their ancestors. As Peter learned more about them, he wondered why it stated beside some of the children's names on the census report, father unknown. He wondered what happened to the father. Was he killed? In jail? Maybe the slave master was the father and they wanted to keep it a secret.

Back then, they would sale the mother, dividing the families. The slave master would load the mother up in a wagon and the children would run beside the wagon as it pulled off, begging the slave master and his workers not to take their mother. The father would be working in the fields or sent to jail, leaving the children to never see their parents again, and sometimes they would even split the children up. Black women cooked and cleaned for their white slave master's families, breastfeeding their babies while they were separated from their own. When the slave master and his family were outside in the heat sitting on the front porch, the black maids would surround them to make sure they stayed cool by fanning them.

At night, the slave master would have one of the black maids to lay across the bed on top of his feet to keep them warm because the house was so big, the wood burning fireplace would only heat a certain area of the house. Their wives weren't fond of their husband's request because eventually it would lead to him inappropriately touching the workers. Black men worked from sun up to sun down in the fields and if they didn't comply, they would be whipped, sold, lynched, beat, or put in jail. Black women were constantly raped, abused, and mistreated by the slave master and his family.

Peter was told about a black maid that had been on her feet cooking and cleaning all day. The slave master's wife came in the kitchen and started to taste the food, she got a fork full of mashed potatoes and didn't like it, so she stabbed the black maid in the eye with her fork. The evil and harsh treatment that black people endured is why many politicians are trying to erase black history from the classrooms, also known as American history. Many white people became filthy rich off the backs of black people. Some are embarrassed and don't want others to know how their ancestors mistreated the black race.

Black people were even punished because they wanted to read and write, wanting a better life for them and their families. White people did everything to make sure black people didn't get the education that they well deserved. They stole land and wealth from the black race and many other races of color, and if they asked about their assets, they were killed. They would make the black men have sex with many women so the slave master will have more slaves. Former U.S. Presidents were known to have black women to serve as maids and men and women as slaves in order to keep their farms thriving. Black people were treated horribly, constantly used and abused. They would beat the hell out of them to make a dollar. The more slaves they had, the more money they made.

Peter knew that the black race had endured a lot but they remained strong and mighty. He believed at an early age if you work hard, you can do and be anything you want to be. Children can become scientists, mathematicians, photographers, police officers, executive producers, teachers, engineers, presidents, artists, doctors, politicians, farmers, architects, social workers, astronomers, actors, actresses, professional athletes, firefighters, authors, counselors, entrepreneurs, chefs, nurses, film directors, accountants, and lawyers. He understood it didn't matter where you came from but where you're going.

Peter reminisced about his grandmother Lena. She was killed on Murry Farm by a storm. A tornado came through and killed a lot of the black slaves. Murry Farm was like a prison farm. The only way you could get off the farm was to run away. If you were sent to jail, they later transported you to Murry Farm. The city was known for falsely accusing black men with rape. They would charge them with a prison sentence but to pay off their debt they became workers at Murry Farm. They trumped up so many charges on black people, once you were sent to the farm, you would never leave unless by death.

White people were known to lie on black men and women to get ahead, in many instances, it is still like that today, however, some uphold integrity, morals and values. The city would make a lot of money in farming. Black men and women worked all day with very few breaks, never getting paid and constantly being mistreated. Stories similar to these caused an outrage within today's society, but you cannot be mad about black history, it is our American history. White people didn't want black people to know how to read and know who they were, fearful that their evil ways would be exposed. They even took books out of the Bible (the Apocrypha), so Black people wouldn't realize that we are the chosen people by God, the Israelites. The Bible, also known as "The Good Book," is a great source of moral guidance, wisdom, inspiration, and comfort in difficult times. Its positive teachings promote love, compassion, and righteousness. It is good to know your history but we must love one another as God loved the church.

Society tries to minimize the contributions the ancestors made and encourage division among black people. Stopping generational curses and changing the narrative of our lives is a powerful journey. Be aware and recognize patterns in your family history. Understanding your beliefs passed down can help you identify with what you want to change. Have faith in your own abilities. Pray and set your own path. You are not your parents or grandparents; their struggles don't have to be your struggles. Educate yourself and learn about the issues that affect your family. This might involve prayer, communicating with family or seeking therapy. Knowledge can empower you to make informed choices. You are not perfect, so stop expecting perfection in others. Have self-reflection, taking time to think about your own values and beliefs.

Journaling can be a helpful tool to explore your thoughts and feelings. Be intentional. Define what a positive future looks like for you. Set specific, achievable goals that align with this vision. Seek support and surround yourself with people who uplift you. Whether it's family, friends, mentors, or support groups, having a network can provide encouragement and guidance. Forgive yourself and others. Letting go of past grievances can be freeing and allows you to move forward.

Pray and ask God for grace and mercy, do something different and create new traditions. Establish new family practices that reflect your morals and ethics. This could be through celebrations, communication styles, or family activities. Professional guidance can provide insights and coping strategies to help break negative cycles. Be kind and treat others how you want to be treated. Practices like meditation, prayer or simply taking time for yourself can enhance your abilities. Change takes time. Celebrate small victories and hang in there, even when it gets challenging.

Remember, you have the power to redefine who you want to be and create a legacy that reflects your goals and aspirations. Use the journey of your ancestors as a motivation to be successful in life. Get an education, buy cattle, land, commercial and residential properties, start a business, invest and save money. Write books to tell your stories, and always know who you are and whose you are. No matter what curve balls life throws your way, be resilient, follow your dreams and never give up.

CHAPTER 10

PETER AND HIS RED BICYCLE

Growing up Peter had many jobs working for Mrs. Bozell and Mrs. Palmer, well-known ladies in the community. At age twelve, Peter washed and waxed floors, manicured and mowed the lawn, washed dishes, windows, cleaned gutters, and ran daily errands. Mrs. Bozell and some of the community men would give Peter money to buy them tobacco and snuff from the corner store. Tobacco is a plant where the leaves are smoked, sniffed, or chewed. Snuff is a type of smokeless tobacco product made from finely ground or shredded tobacco leaves. Moist snuff tobacco is placed in the mouth, usually between the cheek and gum or behind the upper or lower lip. Dry snuff tobacco is inhaled through the nose.

Peter was the errand boy in the community and absolutely loved it. He reminisced how everyone seemed to enjoy Garrett snuff. The women would say, "Peter get the #3 stars or #4 stars," which was the strength of the snuff. The men would tell him, "Peter get me a days' worth of tobacco." Peter didn't understand why the elders loved snuff and tobacco so much. To him, it made your breath stink. The ladies loved Peter and always seemed to want to kiss him on his lips when they were dipping snuff. Sadly, no one knew it back in the day, but both of these substances were addictive and caused cancer.

Peter was an entrepreneur before he knew what the word meant. He worked at a grocery store as a stock clerk, and cleaned the butcher blocks in the meat market. Peter always worked hard and loved the money that he made until one day he had to train a young white guy on his duties at the grocery store. Peter was making seventy-five cents per hour to later find out that the guy he was training was making one dollar per hour. He asked his boss about the difference in pay but was never given a direct answer. He left the topic alone because he knew some money was better than no money and he didn't want to lose his job.

Peter had many side hustles. He would attach a lawn mower, rake, gas can, and hoe to the back of his red bicycle. He rode his bike all over the community asking to cut the grass for homeowners and even businesses. There was an oil business that opened right beside Peter's neighborhood called Phillips 66. At the time, Peter didn't know that the owner of the service station, Bud Allen, was also the owner of the football team, the Houston Oilers. Everyday Mr. Allen would wear a white shirt and khaki pants. Peter would ride his bike to the service station and chat with Mr. Allen. In the conversation, he would market his lawn care business. Peter knew if he started cutting grass for businesses, he would be able to make a lot more money. Unfortunately, Mr. Allen already had a lawn guy for the service station, but it was a breath of fresh air to know that he got a chance to frequently chat with the owner of a nationally known football team.

Peter loved to run and if he wasn't running, he would ride his red bicycle. One day he was riding it so fast he was side by side with a car. Peter yelled, "How fast are we going?" The driver shouted, "We are going 23 mph." He was happy to know he could ride his bike just as fast as a car. Peter was never known for seating still; he was always active and being productive. He was very strong and muscular. The back of his calves in his legs were filled with muscles. He enjoyed riding his bike, running and playing football. When the adults would go to work, he would ride his bike to see his girlfriend Irene who lived in Third Ward. This was a 35-minute car drive but Peter didn't mind, he loved to ride his bike. Even today in his mid 70's, Peter is often seen in his neighborhood riding his bike.

CHAPTER 11

HIGH SCHOOL INTERGRATION

In 1966, Peter attended Stephen F. Austin High School on Dumble Street. He played a major role in integrating the school because he was the first black student to attend. In junior high school Peter started going by his birth name Paul. He didn't realize his name was Paul until he returned back to Houston from Crockett, Texas. He liked his name Paul and was happy when everyone started calling him by his birth name.

Paul was very athletic, a star on the football team and track team. He played defensive safety, did punt returns and kick-offs, often catching and intercepting the ball. Paul was very talented; he played many different positions on the football team. Paul had a strategy; he watched the quarterback's feet very closely and would quickly intercept the ball. He could predict the quarterback's next move based on the position of his feet. Paul was the star of the team which was a blessing and a curse because his football coach relied on him for the win. He was the only black player on the team. Paul was upset that occasionally his teammates missed practice, but he was never allowed to miss a practice because he played on the A team and B team during football practice. Paul excelled at everything in football and everyone on the field depended on him, especially Coach Beasley.

One day Paul decided to take it easy and not play as hard. "Paul, get your black ass in front like you supposed to be!" Coach Beasley yelled. Once Paul was getting ready to intercept the ball and got kneed in the stomach. He fell to the ground, and got the wind knocked out of him. Coach Beasley ran to the field to make sure he was okay. Later that day, Coach Beasley told Paul that he should have hit the opponent low but he hit him high which caused his injury.

Paul was known for being a quick runner, often scoring with interceptions, and when he ran the students and faculty would go crazy screaming, "Go Chocolate Drop! Go Chocolate Drop!" That was Paul's nickname that the coach and his teammates gave him. Paul's newfound fame didn't set well with everyone. One morning as he entered his homeroom classroom, he heard someone whisper, "Hey Nigger!" Paul asked. "Who said that?" When he looked around, he couldn't figure out where it was coming from. The chant, "Hey Nigger" started again and Paul was able to see it was a white football player sitting in the back of the classroom.

Paul walked over to him and asked, "Did you call me a nigger?" He had his head slightly down and didn't respond. "I will get with you this afternoon," Paul exclaimed. Paul was absolutely loved by his teachers and the football staff and team. He couldn't believe that this guy on the team would call him that. Paul went into the locker room that afternoon and confronted the white football player, telling his teammates that he called him a nigger in the classroom.

The football team surrounded the white player and asked, "You called Washington a nigger?" He slumped down on the bench and put his head down. Paul was grateful to see how the football team stood up for him. Thankfully, no one got hurt especially seeing that the white boy wasn't so big and bad like he acted in the classroom. Paul got along with almost everyone and was often invited by his white friends to play football at Stonewall Jackson High School. No one cared about what color you were because they had one thing in common, their love for football. If you got into a disagreement, you talked it out or fought it out and shortly afterwards you went back to playing football.

CHAPTER 12

MR. POPULARITY

Paul was very athletic and full of positivity. At school, he had many girls that adored him, especially the white girls, but he had his heart set on girls that looked just like him. Paul loved black girls and always would refer to the saying, "The blacker the berry the sweeter the juice." He was asked to go to the school dance by his white friends. Although Paul was a great dancer, his white friends thought that all black people knew how to dance. At the dance, Paul was shocked when one of his white friends approached him and asked if he would dance with his girlfriend. "Ok," Paul said nervously. He started dancing with his girlfriend, then here comes another friend asking the same question, then another and another.

Paul didn't realize how much attention he would get at the dance. Before he knew it, all of the girls were lined up and started fussing with each other saying, "He promised that he would dance with me first." "Ok, I will dance with two of you at the same time." Paul explained. He couldn't believe that his teammates agreed to him dancing with their girlfriends. Paul's favorite dance was the Mayfair dance, a popular dance during the mid 1960's in Texas. It was like you were dancing while threading a ribbon with your body, over and under a person. He loved to be pared with a pretty girl when doing this dance.

Later that year, Paul's Hispanic friends invited him to their school dance. He enjoyed it because everyone danced together learning new dances from each other. Paul was very popular in high school. In the hallway, you would hear the guys saying, "Hey Paul!" "Hey Paul!" "What's good soul brother?" Paul had many friends but there were a few jealous ones that called him names under their breath. He never cared about what they said as long as they didn't say it to his face. He was very easygoing unless you crossed him the wrong way.

Paul wore hammy downs during his early childhood, but he was the best dressed in middle school and high school. He loved the layaway plan because he could pay on the items for months. Paul loved wearing suits and sometimes carried a briefcase to school. He had multiple jobs, and in his mind, he was a businessman. Although Paul was popular in school, he didn't always make the best choices and was given a hard time by a few of his teachers. He was threatened by the school's principal that if he made one more mistake, he would not allow him to graduate high school. Paul couldn't take that chance and talked with his mom about transferring to Jack Yates High School. Stephen F. Austin High School was only thirty minutes from their house and he loved the school but he didn't want to risk not graduating.

CHAPTER 13

HIGH SCHOOL SWEETHEART

Paul had a beautiful heart with a kind spirit and was very fond of the girls. He met a nice girl named Irene from Studewood, in the Acres Home community in Northwest Houston. They met in the 10th grade at Jack Yates High School, located in the Third Ward community of Houston, Texas, notable for celebrity graduates like famed actresses Phylicia Rashad and Debbie Allen, recording artist Johnny Nash, journalist Roland Martin, and the late, former star tight end, George Floyd.

Paul would see Irene and her friend Daisy that he had known since elementary school. He thought Irene was cute and every morning before the bell rung, Paul would go and say hello and take his fingers and mess up Irene's bangs. Daisy would yell, "Paul, leave my friend alone!" Irene wouldn't say anything but would give Paul the biggest smile. Everyday Paul would do the same thing, mess up Irene's bangs until he finally got up the nerve to ask her out on a date.

Paul didn't have a car but Irene's family had a 1966 Cadillac that he loved. Irene would come by and pick Paul up and they would go to the movies and out to eat. This was the first car that Paul had ever seen when it approaches another vehicle, it would dim its lights automatically. Paul started to have feelings for Irene and wanted to spend as much time with her as he could. Irene's parents owned a lot of rent houses in the Houston area and Paul would tag along with Irene's family assisting in doing chores to get the rent houses ready for their tenants. Paul was no stranger to hard work and he enjoyed spending quality time with Irene.

Irene was a special girl, and Paul knew she would be a keeper. She was beautiful, family-oriented, kind and loving. She came from a family of hard workers that had a strong faith in God. They loved attending church together and fellowshipping with one another. Paul and Irene often discussed life after high school and they both knew that they wanted to be together.

Paul transferring to Jack Yates High School was the best decision he could ever make, even though he had to take three city buses just to get to school. Sometimes the bus wasn't on time, or the bus was too crowded making him late for school. However, Paul was persistent and decided to hang in there and not quit. Life's choices are the decisions we make that will affect our future and determine our path. From the careers we choose, who we decide to build relationships with, our morals and values, financial obligations, and our decisions dictate our future. With hard work and determination, Paul and Irene graduated together from Jack Yates High School on May 1969.

CHAPTER 14

DRAFTED TO THE VIETNAM WAR

After graduating from high school, Paul was drafted to the United States Army in 1969. He attended basic training and infantry training in Fort Polk, Louisiana. Paul married his high school sweetheart Irene on January 3, 1970. The thought of him leaving his new bride and family behind wasn't in the plan for Paul but for most black men that had even the smallest run in with the law, they were given two choices, to go to jail or get drafted to the military. Paul recalled a black man that he didn't know give him advice when he first joined the military. With authority the man said, "Don't be no hero, that's how you will get killed quick." This played in Paul's head for a very long time and he wholeheartedly took his advice. While in Vietnam, many Vietnamese locals would tell the black soldiers that this wasn't their war to fight, yet most of the men that served on the frontline were African American and Hispanic men.

Paul was a Point Leader (Grunt) in the field, he was responsible for leading the soldiers into battle. Soldiers carried heavy backpacks filled with weapons and supplies, such as, can goods, letters from family members, compasses, sleeping bags, tents or tarps, flameless ration heaters, water canteens, cleaning equipment, flashlights, clothes, first aid kits, packaged military food, rounds of machine gun bullets, and M16 rifles. When the soldiers saw a plane, "The Freedom Bird" as they called it, you would see soldiers being dropped off in Vietnam or they would be taking soldiers back to the, "The World" (United States).

Paul and his comrades would see the planes and fantasize about going home, looking at it until it was out of sight. They would take out their calendars and start yelling, "I got forty-nine more days until I go home!" "I got thirty more days!" "I got twenty more days until I'm headed home!" This gave the soldiers hope that their freedom was near. It was hard living in the jungle, your hygiene was always compromised. The only time you took a bath was if you crossed a river, which could be twenty days or longer.

The soldiers lived in very hostile and dangerous conditions. On the battlefield, soldiers didn't know if they would be alive to see the next second, minute or hour. They could easily get shot or step on a landmine. Some nights soldiers didn't get any sleep if they were on duty. Paul was on duty one night protecting his soldiers when he was startled by a sound in the jungle that appeared to be the enemy. It was dark with very limited light. He listened and could hear the footsteps coming closer and closer. Paul shot his gun in the direction of the sound and thankfully there was immediate silence. He sat very still but felt bad about killing another soldier. When daylight was approaching, Paul shared the incident with his comrades. They laughed and said, "Washington, don't feel bad, this is what you killed last night," holding up a monkey by his tail. Paul was relieved as the jungle was filled with laughter.

There were several incidents where soldiers had to demand respect. Paul had been out in the field for many months, when he had to take care of some personal business in the rural area of Vietnam. Afterwards, he went to the commissary (PX) and ordered a hamburger. When it was ready, the Vietnamese waitress aggressively threw it to him. Paul yelled, "Do I look like a dog? You don't throw a paying customer their food," so he threw it back to her. He was aiming for her face, but thankfully it hit the wall. He was happy it didn't hit her because he didn't want to face any assault charges.

Paul went up to address the incident with the waitress's boss when he noticed they had called the military police. He was given an apology and went back and sat with the other troops. The military police looked at them while holding their guns and without hesitation, Paul and the troops looked back with their M16 rifles on their shoulders. No words were exchanged, the soldiers remained unharmed and they later returned back to the battlefield.

Coming off the helicopter pad, Paul and a few of the brothers were approached by a white lieutenant. The lieutenant said, "I need you all to blouse your boots and get a haircut." This meant to "secure your trousers," which will keep your slacks from flapping in the wind. It kept loose fabrics from catching while jumping out of the aircraft, and it also kept the leeches off your body. Cigarette butts would pull the leeches off but would leave a red mark due to them sucking the blood from your body.

Although it was a valid request made by the lieutenant, they were disturbed by it. Paul wasn't afraid to speak up and get the respect he well deserved. He responded, "You weren't worried about us and how we looked when we were getting our butts shot off in the jungle, sacrificing our lives on the frontline." Paul and four of his comrades had their M16 rifles on their shoulders but in unison decided to lower them. The lieutenant was trying to flex his authority in front of another white lieutenant, but it didn't work, it was two against four. The conversation quickly ended and Paul and the brothers went on their way.

While in Vietnam you are issued a combat uniform with your name, United States Army and grade insignia badges sewn on. It makes you feel good to see your name and credentials, however, you have to wear this same uniform for about four months, leaving soldiers sweaty, dirty, smelly and very uncomfortable. Your undershirt and underwear were so filthy, you ended up throwing them away without getting a replacement. When soldiers had to turn in their old uniform to get a new one, they never saw their old uniform with their name on it again. It wasn't important back in the early 1970s to wear your correct name on your military uniform.

African Americans, Asian Americans, Hispanic Americans, Native Americans, and Caucasians all took part in the Vietnam War. Paul and many other men of color served valiantly on the frontlines during the Vietnam War, facing unique challenges and experiences. Many African American soldiers served in the infantry units, such as the 1st Infantry and 2nd Infantry Divisions, as well as in specialized roles like medics, engineers, and support personnel. They fought alongside their white counterparts, often in some of the most dangerous combat situations. African Americans saw combat at a higher percentage and suffered casualties at a higher rate. Dr. Martin Luther King, Jr. referred to the Vietnam War as a white man's war, and a black man's fight.

In the jungle, tensions would increase day in and day out, because of the constant threat of the enemies. Every day was just another day, the days all seemed the same. You didn't realize that it was a holiday until they would bring special food to the field. In the military, you're given orders but never told the whole truth. Paul and his combat team were told to get in a helicopter, they flew for over 12 hours, landing in Cambodia. Immediately after landing they ran to the rubber trees for cover. Soldiers often lived in makeshift camps or temporary shelters, facing issues with food supply and sanitation. The lack of fresh water and proper facilities exacerbated the challenges of daily life. The fear of hidden enemy forces created an atmosphere of paranoia.

The isolation of the jungle environment and the constant threat of ambush contributed to high levels of stress and anxiety. To put their minds at ease, some soldiers would read, play games, tell dirty jokes and when given the opportunity, some would hire prostitutes to assist with releasing their stress. Paul was happy when he was able to fly to meet his wife Irene in Hawaii. They say that, "Absence makes the heart grow fonder," and they truly made up for lost time. Paul would spoil his wife by buying all the latest fashions, and wouldn't forget about himself buying nice tailored suits and gator shoes.

Many African American soldiers claimed that they were unfairly targeted for punishment, including being denied for promotion and disproportionately assigned menial tasks. African Americans soldiers would complain that they were discriminated against in promotions because they stayed in the same grade too long. They would teach the white trainees and pretty soon their trainees pass them by and would get the promotion. African American soldiers faced racism both in the military and from the broader society. Sadly, this type of treatment is still going on in America today. They often dealt with segregation in units and discrimination from fellow soldiers, which added to the stress of combat. Racial tensions created internal divisions, causing African American soldiers and other soldiers of color to sometimes refuse to fight.

Black culture and norms were also not initially acknowledged on bases. Some African American troops did not have access to black haircare products, soul music tapes, nor books or magazines about black culture and history. Instead, on the radio they mostly played country music by white artists. Military barbers had no formal training on experience cutting black hair. Thankfully, military leadership took some action to make black troops feel more included, adding more diverse music in the clubs, hiring black bands, dancers and black entertainers to perform. Bases began to stock black haircare products and garments like dashikis, while books about black culture and history were added to base libraries.

The enlistment rate for African Americans were high, and they made up a significant percentage of combat troops, often exceeding their population percentage in the United States. This was partly due to economic factors and limited opportunities in civilian life. Over 7,000 African Americans died in the Vietnam War more than any other race. Some military leaders believed that African Americans did not have the physical, mental or moral character to withstand warfare but they were placed on the front lines and were commonly relegated to labor-intensive service positions. However, many Black servicemen became leaders within their units and organized groups against discrimination. Their experiences in the military sometimes fueled their involvement in the Civil Rights Movement upon returning home. Paul and many others received numerous commendations and awards for their bravery and service, with many demonstrating exceptional courage in battle. Paul's military service granted him the opportunity to receive a recognition letter from Former President Barack Obama.

The war was filled with physical labor, emotional and mental strain. The casualties of this long war, from both sides, were extensive and brutal due to guerilla warfare and the use of chemical weapons. United States troops bombed key industrial supply sites in the North while under the constant threat of the longing massive search operations in the South. Half a million Americans were in Vietnam fighting nearly 300,000 North Vietnamese regulars and Viet Cong Guerillas. Dead enemy bodies were the measure of success.

Paul dealt with numerous health issues in the jungle, including heat exhaustion, dehydration, and tropical diseases like malaria and dengue fever. The presence of leeches and insects added to the discomfort. He was very sick and almost died suffering from a high fever of 106 due to malaria and had to be air-lifted by helicopter for care. After many weeks, he recovered, however, his military leaders requested for him to resume his duties on the frontline. Thankfully he was recommended by medical professionals that after his illness and serving two years in Vietnam, it was time for him to return back home to the United States.

Paul flew to Hawaii then to Vietnam on Pan Am Airlines and returned back home on United Airlines. Soldiers in the battlefield hadn't seen American women for many months, and if they saw American women, it was in the military hospitals and clinics. Paul and other military soldiers being in their early twenties and thirties were excited to see the young and beautiful flight attendants. They looked forward to their warm smiles, kindness, and of course those short mini-skirts. After the tensions of war, the thrill of seeing beautiful faces were something the soldiers looked forward to. Instead, to their surprise, they only saw old, weary and wrinkled, nearly retired flight attendants that were the age of their parents on their flight.

African Americans were promised freedom, equality and a good living but after the Vietnam War most of them only dealt with a hard time. The American dream was available for only a select few. African American men played a crucial role in the Vietnam War, navigating both the complexities of combat and the challenges of racial inequality. Paul served on the frontline in the Vietnam War from 1969 – 1971. He was medically discharged and successfully ended his time in the United States Army, ranked as a E-4 (Specialist 4). Paul was awarded many prestigious awards and honors for his heroism, sacrifice and service.

CHAPTER 15

WHAT HAPPENED TO THE AMERICAN DREAM?

When Paul returned back to the states, he was faced with a lot of hardships. He sacrificed his life for his country but what happened to his American dream? It was hard for him as a war veteran to find a decent job making enough money to support his family. Paul fought for his country but didn't feel that his country fought for him. He served on the front, but his country didn't have his back. Paul worked as a machine shop operator, but shortly had to quit because he wasn't making enough to make ends meet. He later worked as a bus operator for Rapid Transit making $1.60, working from 4:00 AM – 6:00 PM daily, it was hard for Paul, especially dealing with injuries from the war.

Paul was happily married to his wife Irene, who supported him in every way that she could, which allowed them to become homeowners at age 21. He wanted to make sure that his wife and children lived in a home, not rent houses or an apartment as he had growing up. Homeownership was a big deal to Paul and his family. Irene gave birth to their first born, a daughter named Tanya. She was a good baby, very sweet, polite and truly daddy's little girl. When she got older and got into mischief, all Paul needed to do was shake his belt at her and she quickly straightened up.

Years later their son Michael was born. Him and Paul enjoyed playing basketball together. Michael loved riding his bike just like his daddy. Michael was a true character, when he got a whooping, he always acted like he was hyperventilating. Once Michael and his friends got caught on MLK Blvd. Paul had told his son time and time again not to cross the street into another neighborhood. Michael saw his daddy driving up and he immediately fell in the ditch still on his bike attempting to hide. "Didn't I tell you not to cross this busy street. What if you had gotten hit by a car?" Paul asked. Paul realized that all bad things that your children do don't always require a whooping, sometimes a firm talk is all the discipline that they need. After their talk, Michael learned his lesson.

Averill was the baby of the bunch. He was the biggest flirt. At age six, he would sit in Paul's lap honking the horn of his 18-wheeler truck while blowing kisses to the ladies as they passed by. Paul and his boys loved playing basketball in the backyard. He always did a great hook shot but Averill and Michael would accuse their daddy of cheating. Basketball was their favorite game and the boys would be waiting on their daddy to come home from work to play. Paul loved his children dearly and adored his Godson Fredinand, who began staying with him and Irene shortly after their daughter Tanya was born. Paul was the father figure that Fredinand needed. He was a great big brother for Tanya and helper to Paul and Irene. Paul was grateful to be blessed with a beautiful wife and kids.

Paul was very kind and had a heart for single mothers, it was like he was the neighborhood dad. When he saw the children of single mothers waiting at the bus stop to catch the city bus to go to school, Paul would pick them up in his van because they attended the same school as his children. His children didn't like that their daddy did this almost every morning, but Paul remembered as a child he had to take three different city buses in Houston to get to his school every morning. Sometimes it was scary for Paul being in the buses with adults working downtown. He would be tired before even arriving to school just from waiting at the bus stop.

Many traumas followed Paul throughout his life after serving in the war. He often experienced nightmares in the middle of the night, which occasionally kept his wife Irene up. It wasn't easy being married to a war veteran because you never know what event could set off their triggers. As a spouse to a soldier in battle you had to have tough skin, taking care of the family, and constantly worrying if you may get a phone call or visit on your doorstep with bad news. Thankfully Irene stayed prayerful and was showered by her family's love. While in the military, Paul was exposed to Agent Orange, a powerful herbicide used by U.S. military forces during the Vietnam War to eliminate forest cover and crops for North Vietnamese and Viet Cong troops. The U.S. program, codenamed Operation Ranch Hand, sprayed more than 20 million gallons of various herbicides over Vietnam, Cambodia and Laos from 1961 to 1971.

Agent Orange, which contained the deadly chemical dioxin, was the most commonly used herbicide. It was later proven to cause serious health issues—including cancer, birth defects, rashes and severe psychological and neurological problems—among the Vietnamese people, as well as returning U.S. servicemen and their families. Agent Orange affected Paul and many other soldiers in the military. Paul is healthy but continues to suffer with hypertension, diabetes, neuropathy, eye problems, hearing loss and other disabilities.

Besides health issues, after returning back home, Paul continued dealing with being offered low paying jobs. He rarely landed a position that paid him what he was worth. He was hired at Central Freight Line as a truck driver and although it didn't pay much, it was a job to help pay the bills. One day he wore his Vietnam boonie hat to work when his boss approached him and stated, "I suggest you not wear that hat to work again." This was very disturbing to Paul because he had seen his white co-worker wear his cowboy hat every day and never got scolded. There was no respect for veterans, especially an African American veteran and Paul knew with the low pay and lack of respect, this job would be short-lived.

Months later, Paul interviewed at Yellow Freight and got the job! He was happy because it paid more money but every day he was watched like a hawk by his boss and co-workers. Black and Hispanic men worked harder than any other race but weren't respected and often was looked down upon. Paul remembered unloading his truck on the dock when he heard a voice ask, "Are you a security guard?" The guy started quickly walking down the dock, "Hey! Hey! Hey you! You didn't hear me calling you?" He asked. Paul explained, "I heard you say, Hey! Hey you! My name is Paul Washington." The lack of respect that a black man faced, especially being a war veteran was sickening. Paul was a hard-working man just looking for his American dream to support his family but continued to struggle.

Years later he drove trucks for a local grocery chain, and although this job seemed to be promising, he soon found out that the company's rules didn't apply to everyone. Paul was a jack of all trades, he knew what hard work looked like as early as six-years-old but continued to struggle in the workforce, always being overworked and underpaid. There were many other jobs that Paul had but because of his injuries, it posed a lot of conflict. Paul dealt with this struggle for many years which wayed heavily on him and his family. Working as a truck driver for Safeway, a popular grocery chain was the best job for Paul because employees were treated with kindness and respect, and it had great benefits and pay. He enjoyed his new job, because it allowed him to meet new people when he made his deliveries to the different store locations.

After working for Safeway, Paul was happy to get a small taste of the American dream for him and his growing family but sometimes it still wasn't enough to make ends meet. After many closed doors with getting his full military benefits, Paul developed a love for the street life, often hanging out with friends and doing the unimaginable to help him ease his pain. Paul wasn't a drinker or smoker, but absolutely loved to flirt and dance with the women. He had been known for his dancing skills since middle school. Although his intentions with hanging out with the fellas were pure at first, and was a way for him to release stress, being in certain environments and hanging with the wrong people will influence negative behaviors.

Paul was brought up in the church but failed to seek God within his marriage. He found himself in situations that led him to not honor his marriage vows. Paul loved his wife and children deeply but the constant let downs of life and curiosities forced him into a lifestyle of wild and crazy escapades. Sadly, after many years of marriage Paul and Irene got a divorced. He moved into a one-bedroom apartment with a black and white TV, China cabinet, and a few other bare necessities. Paul knew that Irene was a wonderful wife and mother to their children, but when God is not a priority in your life and you think as the saying goes, "The grass is greener on the other side," you make irrational decisions that lead to you losing everything you worked hard for. Paul quickly learned that there was nothing in those streets for him but trouble.

Years later Paul met a lady named Jo Ann at a truck stop in Hempstead, Texas. They begin a friendship that turned into a serious relationship and later he was blessed with two more sons, Jason and Quincy. Both boys were very smart, handsome and loved playing basketball and riding their bikes in the neighborhood like their older brothers. Paul didn't know how to introduce his boys that he had with Jo Ann to their other siblings, but one day, out of the blue, Tanya asked her dad if they had any other siblings. Paul realized that this was the outlet that he needed to bring the siblings together. He made arrangements with the moms for the siblings to meet, and thankfully Jason and Quincy were welcomed with opened arms by their siblings and his ex-wife Irene. Although Paul and Irene divorced, they continued to have a lasting friendship for the sake of their children.

CHAPTER 16

HELP OUR VETERANS

Going to the VA hospital was not an easy journey. For years, Paul would get denied his full benefits after serving in the military. It started with receiving only 10% of his government benefits, then 20%, 30% and increased slightly each year. He was drafted into the United States Army in 1969 and medically discharged from the Army in 1971 but didn't receive 100% of his benefits until 2009, 38 years later. While serving in Vietnam, Paul remembered getting a call from his wife Irene when he was serving active duty because there was a problem with her not receiving the checks from the government. As a soldier fighting for his country, on the frontline, the government didn't make it a priority to compensate the families for Paul and many other men of color. How can you fight, sacrifice and serve on the frontline for your country but in return they don't fight for you and your family? These were questions Paul thought about often.

At the VA, Paul would sit and watch how the veterans struggled on the process of getting the assistance that they needed. Some were purple heart soldiers, which meant they earned a badge of honor for their courage and bravery, being injured in the military. Paul would watch how some veterans could barely walk but never offered a wheelchair or scooter. These men suffered after being discharged. Some couldn't find a job, housing, on top of dealing with medical illnesses, like, hearing loss, migraines, mental illnesses, depression, grief and sadness, injuries, and loss of limbs.

Paul didn't hesitate to assist the veterans, often offering them his own personal cane, walker and scooter. Most didn't know the process because it was a lot of paperwork, phone calls and follow-ups needed, and you had to have a doctor for every different illness. Communication played a big part in not receiving benefits for some of the Spanish speaking veterans. Many struggled because of lack of communication, not knowing where to start. Paul would look for a Spanish speaking staff member or direct them to the bilingual phone line. What irritated Paul the most was the doctors he was sent to lacked empathy and compassion. They had no clue what the soldiers endured, especially being on the frontline, but yet they were the ones to determine the benefits that the soldiers would receive.

Paul felt pre-judged before he even began to speak to his doctor. It was like black men and other men of color were looking for a handout. When you meet with your doctor, you should never speak with intelligence or wear a suit and look good while requesting benefits, because you will definitely get denied. Although it was Paul's style to dress for success and wear a suit, at the VA he settled for un-ironed jeans and a t-shirt. Most of the doctors were white men, going directly by what was written in the medical books. Paul communicated the atrocities that the soldiers had to deal with on the frontline with them but they showed no empathy, it was like they heard the teacher from Charlie Brown......Wah, wah, wah, wah." Paul didn't feel seen or heard when he had to meet with his doctors at the VA, for years getting denied for his full benefits.

It was difficult for Paul having to provide for him and his family, and when he finally got a job, it was hard transitioning to the civilian life working a 9-5 job. A lot of veterans needed disability benefits because they couldn't keep up with the job requirements like a civilian worker, due to their illnesses and injuries. Some veterans witnessed so much trauma that they had mental health issues but were only a given a hotline number to call if they had suicidal thoughts. These veterans needed prayer, immediate therapy, a daily advocate or friend to help them adjust to civilian life.

Although there are agencies available, and it does save lives to call for help, if you are having suicidal thoughts, when you are facing trauma, you want the pain to end, and an 800-number may be the last thing on your mind. As an American citizen of the United States serving in the military, there should be equal opportunity to achieve success and prosperity through quality living, with good paying jobs, upper to middle-income housing, and a steady cash-flow. Again, where was the American dream for the African American veterans and other veterans of color?

At the VA, soldiers sat in the waiting room for hours without a clue of what to do. Paul was blessed with a beautiful spirit, becoming the waiting room's benefits advocate directing the veterans of the steps to take. Many veterans assumed he worked for the VA because he was very attentive, knowledgeable and patient. Paul witnessed some of the veterans getting frustrated with the workers and the workers tempers flaring with the veterans. It was difficult because a lot of the veterans were old, sick, and didn't know what questions to ask to get the help that they needed.

Oftentimes, their attitudes and lack of respect contributed to not receiving the assistance from the workers. Paul had empathy for both the veterans and workers. In some instances, Paul became the mediator between the two, often apologizing to the workers for the veteran's rude behavior. He understood their frustration, serving in a war for their country, transitioning back into the world, not feeling appreciated for the service and sacrifices you and your family have made, and then, your benefits are denied or the percentage is so low, and as the head of the household, you're struggling to make ends meet.

You couldn't tell the health struggles that Paul faced on a daily basis. Society will sometimes judge others on what they see on the outside. One evening, Paul parked at a handicap parking spot in a shopping center the same time as a white male driver. Paul parked and got out of his vehicle, when the white male driver yelled, "That was my spot! How can you park there? You don't look handicap." Paul was registered as a Veteran with disabilities, which deemed him as handicap. His vehicle displayed a handicap sticker and he was wearing his Vietnam Veteran hat.

Some days Paul could walk like a regular civilian and other days he could not due to his injuries in the war. Although Paul didn't dwell on his diagnosis, when necessary, he parked where he well deserved. All battles aren't meant for us to fight but Paul thought, "The nerve of this man to judge me when he knew nothing about me." As the saying goes, "Kill them with kindness." Although Paul had a few choice words in his head to tell that driver, every action doesn't require a reaction. Paul gave him a smirk and continued to mind his own business as he enjoyed a day of shopping.

Paul reminisced about meeting a 97-year-old veteran at his church during Memorial Day weekend. He was a wise man with a sharp mind, serving for many years in the Korean War. He told Paul that his experience with the VA was quite similar to a lot of veterans. After many years of denials, he finally received 100% of his benefits but it was through his faith, blood, sweat and tears that he was approved. He added that it was a horrible experience for him but many veterans should know that it takes patience, hard work and persistence to get through the process because deep down the government wants you to get denied, delayed, and die so they won't have to pay you or your family the benefits you are owed. Paul couldn't believe what he was hearing but knew it was the absolute truth because he lived it. It may not be the same today as it was back then, but Paul realized whether it was past or present, working for the VA is a very tough job and you must have a heart for the elderly and especially veterans.

CHAPTER 17

DO'S AND DON'TS TO ASK A VETERAN

Besides "Thank you for service," there are many conversations that civilians want to have with Veterans. It is important to know what topics to discuss because some questions could possibly be a trigger that a Veteran may choose not to relive. Being on the frontline in the Vietnam War, Paul witnessed a lot of horrific events that causes a person to experience emotional, physical, and psychological traumas. Through Paul's steadfast faith, family support and strength he was able to conquer his experiences and not allow them to bombard his thinking.

As a Veteran, you get to participate in many speaking engagements and community events. Paul has traveled all over the United States to speak about his experience serving on the frontline in the Vietnam War. He was excited to be invited to a Veterans recognition program and parade at Robison Elementary School in Cypress, Texas by his two little friends Nylah, a 4th grader and her little brother Nalin, a 2nd grader.

The school rolled out the red carpet for the veterans with a complimentary breakfast, indoor parade and recognition program to honor the hard work, dedication, and service the veterans contributed to their country. Paul was elated to be able to represent his friends and speak to their classes about his time serving in the Army. Service men and women are one-of-a kind and work hard to make sure that everyone can continue to enjoy their freedom. Paul highlights a few helpful tips from his experience when conversing with a veteran.

Things Not to Ask a Veteran from Paul's Experiences

Have you ever killed anybody? Are you disable? Do you have Post Traumatic Stress Disorder (PTSD)? Have you ever been shot? Questions like these could make the war veteran have flashbacks and relive aspects of a traumatic event or feel that the event is currently happening. It will cause them to become suicidal, overwhelmed with emotions, feel unsafe or helpless, lose hope for the future, unable to make rational decisions, become depressed, or resort to violence.

Don't judge a veteran by what he or she wears, how they walk or talk, or their lack of resources. It is hard for veterans to adjust back to civilian life. Many will take a dirty, low-paying job rather than no job and risk homelessness. Paul and many other veterans often get frustrated with civilians because the Memorial Day holiday seems to no longer be commemorated for the soldiers that have passed away. Instead, they use their day off work for the purpose of going to the beach, grilling, or shopping for Memorial Day sales. Memorial Day should be designated to mourn and honor its deceased service men and women and to support their families.

Paul is a veteran but also serves as an advocate for veterans speaking at churches, schools, and community events throughout the United States. He wants veterans to know that you're not alone, even if you feel like you are. You can always speak with a trusted loved one, doctor, therapists, another veteran, neighbor, psychologist or minister. When you feel like giving up or feel overwhelmed by emotions, try to focus on getting through the next minute, hour, or day and seek professional help when needed.

Things to Help a Veteran from Paul's Experiences

Give veterans an opportunity to tell their stories. Be patient, kind and listen.

Offer a job with good benefits and pay, let them know if someone you know is hiring. Get involved with a community organization for veterans.

Assist a veteran in finding resources like jobs, food, clothing, shelter and help the ones who are homeless. Volunteer with food shelters to help a veteran. Provide a service dog for a veteran.

Ask a veteran if they have any advice for others transitioning out of the military. Always show love, respect and kindness to a veteran.

Try to find a doctor with a military background that have served so they can better understand what the veteran has been through.

Veterans must understand that you have to file for each illness you are going through such as, hearing, seeing, mental illness, neuropathy, grief and depression, hypertension, paralysis, etc. Seek a veteran advocate for assistance.

Volunteer to transport veterans to and from their VA medical appointments, help veterans understand what benefits they qualify for. Arrange outings for a veteran, assist them with networking with family and friends, this will help with their depression.

A lot of veterans have disabilities that are unknown to the public. Some may be seen with a cane but require a wheelchair. Be available to assist whenever possible.

It is beneficial to learn about mental health conditions before you talk with a veteran. The knowledge you gain can help you understand the veteran's experiences and kind of care they may need. If you feel that your veteran loved one needs help, get the support and treatment that they may need as soon as possible to prevent the symptoms from getting worse.

U.S. military veterans need educating, coaching, and mentoring to help through the confusing VA disability claim process. Ideally veterans need someone with kindness, great communication, highly motivated individuals who demonstrate integrity, empathy, resourcefulness, heart and hustle for veterans.

CHAPTER 18

FINDING THE LOVE OF MY LIFE

Paul and his best friend Brian worked at a trucking company together for many years. He was invited to his friend's wedding when he spotted a beautiful young woman sitting at his table at the wedding reception. Karen was her name, accompanied by her cute little daughter Nyishia. Surprisingly, Karen was the best friend of the bride. Paul quickly sparked up a conversation with her. His interests grew as he politely asked her if she was at the wedding with her husband.

When Karen answered, she was no longer married, this was the green light that Paul needed to get to know her better. Paul felt a strong connection with Karen. He was getting ready to get some refreshments when he asked her and her daughter if they wanted anything. Karen didn't but he was happy to bring back her daughter Nyishia some tasty wedding appetizers. Paul admired Karen and her daughter and offered his phone and pager number to keep in touch.

Although Karen didn't call Paul right away, he was happy to hear from her when he did and asked her out on a date. Their first date was at a fine dining restaurant in Humble, Texas, and a drive to the Wall of Water in the Galleria area in Houston. It was a beautiful start to a friendship sealed with a kiss on the cheek. Paul had a country house in Kendleton, Texas where him and Karen enjoyed spending quality time together. As their relationship began to grow stronger and stronger Paul knew that Karen was the one, and she was interested in building a new life with him. He enjoyed spending time with Karen and her family.

Their courtship didn't last very long. When a man knows what he wants it doesn't take long to make a decision. He met with Karen's father and mother to get permission to marry their daughter and after 6 months of dating, Paul and Karen got married at the courthouse in Humble, Texas. **Proverbs 18:22,** "He who finds a wife finds a good thing, and obtains favor from the Lord." Paul always wanted that special person to love and love him. He had been married multiple times but he finally got it right with Karen because of his strong relationship with God. He admits his first wife was a great wife and mother but because of his love for street life he didn't realize what he had until it was gone. Thankfully, they have maintained many years of love and friendship for the sake of their children, grandchildren and great-grandchildren.

Although Paul's second and third marriages were short-lived, he recognized later in life that all of his previous marriages failed because his first priority wasn't God. When you have a strong relationship with God, read and follow his word, pray and surround yourself around people of good character, you walk and talk differently. You clearly understand your role as a husband and wife. Rely on God. God gives you direction, not the world. **Ephesians 5:25**, "Husbands and wives are called to love one another and treat one another well."

Paul believes that single men and married men should not hang together because married men may start mimicking ways like their single friends. God shows you how to be a good husband and man. Stop following the teachings of the world but follow God. He will direct your path. The Bible is your guide on how to be a caring and loving husband. A good family is a spiritual family and Paul found out that this was where he needed to be. He was happy when him and Karen found a good, Bible-based church home where they attended Sunday school, church and weekly Bible study. Paul has been a member for nearly 25 years, becoming a Deacon and Sunday School Superintendent of Bread of Life Baptist Church in Humble, Texas, where Reverend R.M. Harris is his good friend and pastor.

God's way is always the best way, he is an all-knowing God. He sees what's ahead and knows all of the ramifications of your path. Unlike us, God cannot make mistakes. When you do it God's way, he will pour out an overflow of blessings. Paul is thankful that through his obedience and hard work, God has allowed him to enjoy the fruits of his labor. He loves his wife, children, grandchildren, and great-grandchildren, and is absolutely blessed to be able to be alive to see their accomplishments.

Paul is grateful to be able to stay in a good neighborhood with good friends like Willard and his wife Melinda, who lives next door. Paul and Willard are more like brothers than neighbors, often cutting each other's grass, going to breakfast together, cooking for one another, and helping each other with home improvements after a storm. As a veteran, Paul is very thankful that God helped him to become a better man. He and Karen have been happily married for thirty-three years. Paul's message to all families is to hook up with the ultimate power source, God. The best teaching to give your family is spiritual teaching along with quality time, financial stability and love.

2 Chronicles 7:14, "If my people who belong to me will humbly pray, seek my face, and turn from their wicked ways, then I will hear from heaven, forgive their sin, and heal their land."

CHAPTER 19

FAMILY IS EVERYTHING

Spending time with family and friends is one of Paul's favorite things to do. He enjoys telling jokes and making them laugh. From having quiet conversations at home, to taking his grandchildren and great-grandchildren to march in the Veterans Day parade, going to church, on a vacation or eating at their favorite restaurant, in their eyes, he is, "The World's Greatest Paw-Paw!" Paul has thirteen grandchildren, and two great-grandchildren (twins).

One of his older grandsons had a tattoo created of him on his right forearm. Although Paul wasn't a big fan of tattoos, he was honored and grateful of his grandson's gesture. Having regular family time helps you learn from one another, lowers your stress levels, creates lifelong memories, strengthens emotional bonds and well-being, better your mental health, and gives you a greater sense of purpose. Paul understands that quality time spent with his family is very important as he teaches valuable life lessons that cultivates a nurturing environment and fosters healthy and fulfilling relationships.

Paul didn't feel his mom's love growing up. He knew that she dealt with many traumas that allowed her to take it out on him and others. A lot of black families didn't discuss their pain and hardships, it was something that you didn't talk about, however, when you don't seek help, it could trigger PTSD (Post-Traumatic Stress Disorder), anxiety, depression, nightmares, negativity, health issues, mood swings and create difficulties in relationships.

Paul got introduced to working at an early age, it was his saving grace. He believed if a young boy asks to wash your car, cut your grass, or trim the hedges, you should let him, because it builds confidence, good character and strong work ethics. You should also pay him more than what he asked for. This will help him to do his very best, understand responsibility and stay productive. Both boys and girls should be given new opportunities to learn and grow.

Paul loves his family. He learned a lot from his siblings throughout his life. His older brother Marvin served in the Vietnam War twice before Paul was drafted. Paul and his siblings were raised to have a close relationship and told to always look out for one another. His parents taught them how to be kind and respectful to their elders. When you instill great things in your children at a young age, it will follow them throughout life. He is grateful to be able to share wisdom and spend time with his family.

Children don't ask to be born and it is important to keep a strong relationship with them even if the relationship with their mom or dad doesn't work out. Always be known as a promise-keeper. No matter how small the promise is, no matter who you make the promise to, always keep your word. If plans change that are beyond your control, have open communication, engage in tough conversations with love and empathy. Give respect to get respect, nurture meaningful relationships through good and challenging times.

Humility is knowing that sometimes we are stronger together than apart. Be consistent in your dealings with others. **Luke 6:31,** "Do to others as you would have them do to you." God made Paul a better man, he understands the importance of family, faith, and forgiveness. He loved his mom and forgave her for how she treated him as a child. It can be difficult to forgive when we feel like the person who hurt us needs to be held accountable for their actions.

Forgiveness encourages compassion, unforgiveness encourages bitterness. **Ephesians 4:32**, "Be kind to one another, tenderhearted, forgiving one another, as God in Christ forgave you." Paul and his siblings took turns spending quality time with their mom until she got ill and passed away in 2023. He and his siblings were blessed to make beautiful memories with their mom for ninety-three years.

CHAPTER 20

WISE WORDS FROM A VIETNAM VETERAN

God has truly blessed Paul and his family and he is grateful for his grace and mercy. That's why he gives him all the glory, honor and praise. As a veteran, life wasn't easy for Paul but no matter how hard it got, trusting in God and never giving up allowed him to keep moving forward. Although he experienced excruciating pain, trauma and abuse as a child, he never let his past dictate his future. Forgiveness is the key to not staying stagnant and being able to get the blessing that God has for you. Having a strong relationship with God helped Paul realize that trouble don't last always.

Paul encourages you to go to church, pray, read your Bible and keep God's commandments. "Trust in the Lord with all thine heart; and lean not into thine own understanding. In all thy ways acknowledge him and he shall direct thy paths." **Proverbs 3:5-6**. Jesus reveals himself, "I am Alpha and Omega, the beginning and the end, the first and the last." **Revelation 22:13**. Jesus Christ died on the cross for our sins. Give him praise in the good and bad times.

Your friends may persuade you to make decisions that you know are wrong. Stop listening to people. Put your trust in God and not in man. If they are your true friends, they won't put you in compromising situations to get you in trouble. True friends want to see you do good. Don't be judgmental of others. Paul recalled being very judgmental when he was younger. His pastor had to sit him down and talk to him about his behavior. You never know what others are going through. You will be judge while you're judging others. **Matthew 7:1-5** "Judge not, that you be not judged. For with the judgment, you pronounce you will be judged, and with the measure you use it will be measured to you. Why do you see the speck that is in your brother's eye, but do not notice the log that is in your own eye? Or how can you say to your brother, let me take the speck out of your eye, when there is the log in your own eye. You hypocrite, first take the log out of your own eye, and then you will see clearly to take the speck out of your brother's eye."

Growing up, Paul's family didn't have much but his parents taught them about faith, hard work, responsibility, kindness, compassion and love. Stop complaining about what you don't have and celebrate what you do have. There is no luck in life, it is all blessings from God. As a young man, being drafted and serving on the frontline in the United States Army in the Vietnam War, Paul's journey didn't stop after he was medically discharged, it was just the beginning. It was hard for a war veteran, especially being a black man adjusting in society. The American dream didn't exist for him and many other men and women of color because of lack of jobs, housing and financial security.

Many veterans could have settled to be homeless, but most knew they had families to depend on them. Veterans worked low-paying jobs like, washing windows, cutting grass, cleaning gutters, shining shoes, and doing janitorial work, it was what they had to do to keep food on their tables. We were thankful that God had blessed us to earn a good living and provide the necessities for our families. Everything was not in our timing but God's timing. We worked hard, trusted God and did what we had to do, so later in life God would bless us to do what we wanted to do. Paul reminisced about being asked to talk to students preparing to graduate from high school. The questions were posed, would he recommend the military?

Paul stated, "There's always pros and cons in any situation. If you are interested in joining the military, get your college degree first to be able to have a higher ranking, it will allow you to have positions in leadership and authority. Many men and women of color experienced a great deal of racism in the military. When you are drafted in the military at a lower ranking you are more likely to be bullied and a victim of racism."

Paul talked about being disrespected by guys from Alabama and Mississippi. He stated, "Other criteria that may help you gain authority is if you were in ROTC in high school, you can use your knowledge to train others and get promoted to a squad leader ranking. Being in the military may be a struggle without some college, college degree or ROTC. Nothing in life comes easy. Young people must work harder and smarter to earn what they have."

Paul is very involved in his church and was asked what he would say to a young adult who wants to increase their faith, become a member of a good Bible based church, but feel that the church is hypocritical? "You should always remember that the heart of faith is about your relationship with God, not the flaws of individuals. When judgment day comes God doesn't care what others do, but what did you do. No one is perfect and not all churches are the same. Look for a community that emphasizes grace, love, and genuine growth.

Remember that everyone, including church members, is a work in progress, and may make mistakes. Reading the Bible, praying, and reflecting on your beliefs can strengthen your faith, regardless of the church environment. When you find a church that resonates with you, consider volunteering or participating in small groups. Being involved can help you connect with others who share your faith journey and create a more positive experience.

Paul adores his five children, Tanya, Michael, Averill, Jason, Quincy, Godson Fredinand and Step-daughter Nyishia. It is important to Paul to maintain an active and supportive role in the lives of his family. When asked what makes a good parent? Paul stated, "Parents have to be good role models and instill in their children the importance of responsibility and accountability. Teach your children about God and show them compassion and love." Say things like, "I am proud of you!" "You are doing a good job!" "I love you!" These gestures help you to boost their self-esteem and create a closer bond.

Make your children a priority and be willing to adjust your schedule to spend quality time together. Using profanity or belittling your children is not necessary when scolding them for bad behavior. Parents should talk to their children, not at their children. Some children may only require a firm conversation whereas others may need physical discipline. Never chastise when you are angry, this may cause you to become outraged and you may lose control of the situation. Be mindful that your tone of voice, body language, and every expression is being watched by your children.

Parents are children's first teachers. Always honor thy mother and thy father. Children should always respect and obey their parents or there will be consequences. They must be taught this at an early age. Don't laugh and engage in them having bad behavior when they are young, because when they are older it won't be funny anymore. Teach them right from wrong, set rules and boundaries for your children and stop being their friends. Say what you mean, and mean what you say. When a parent makes a decision, that's it, no negotiating with the children. Giving them money and buying them material things is not the only way to show them love.

If you purchase a car for your child, teach them about the upkeep of the car. Teach them how to fix a flat tire, change the oil, put gas in it, keep it clean and take it to the dealerships for a routine check. Spend time helping with homework, taking them to the park, get them involved with church and youth activities, have a sit-down dinner together, participate in sports and school events.

As young adults, be productive and don't cut corners in life always looking for the easy way out. Learn to get an early start to your day, always do your best, and don't put off what you can do today for tomorrow. Our youth may be able to walk faster but the elders know the road. Keep God first, and he'll work all things together for your good. Paul's life is a testament of what God can do, and what he did for him, he will surely do for you.

ACKNOWLEDGMENTS

I give God all the glory, honor and praise for making me who I am today and blessing me with wisdom and kindness in my heart.

Thank you to my beautiful wife Karen Washington for your everlasting love and support.

To my children, Tanya, Michael, Averill, Jason, Quincy, Godson Fredinand and Step-daughter NyIshia, I am thankful that God has blessed me to be in your lives.

Thank you to my siblings, Marvin, Carl, Angela, and Norma for loving me and being my first best friends. Thank you to all of my family and friends for your support.

To my neighbor and best friend Willard Esters Jr. and family, your brotherhood and love is greatly appreciated. Thank you for always looking out for me and my family.

A great appreciation to my book publishers, DeMorris & LaWanda Burrell with SUSU Entertainment LLC for your many years of support, guidance and dedication in putting my life's journey together to create my book.

Many thanks to my church family and Pastor Reginald M. Harris of Bread of Life Baptist Church in Humble, TX, who is an awesome teacher and has helped me to stay grounded.

Deacon Claude Harris, Deacon Darryl Bryant, Sister Valrie Washington thank you for your encouragement and guidance on my spiritual journey.

Thank you to Debra Blacklock-Sloan, Melrita Taylor, LaWanda Lewis Burrell and members of the African American Library Gregory Friends, for your friendship, support and encouragement.

Thank you to my veteran friend Rossie Nance. We have stuck together since the Vietnam War, 1st Cav 2-5. I'm grateful to my veteran organizations and all the veterans that have served and sacrificed for their country.

To the readers of my book, I pray that my story will bless you with unwavering faith, hope, love and forgiveness today, tomorrow and forevermore.

LETTER TO MY DADDY

Dear Daddy,

Thank you for being my real-life hero. My first words were DA-DA-DA—DA!!! As I've gotten older, to this day, I'm teased for my known phrase, "I'm gonna tell my Daddy!" I always knew you would show up and protect me. You don't play about your ONLY DAUGHTER and I don't play about MY DADDY! I have what most girls want from their father and that's to be spoiled, loved and protected. Nobody could outdo my daddy in my eyes. My Daddy was the strongest soldier, best truck driver, basketball player, wrestler and fighter.

You've not only been an amazing father to your own children, but also a father figure to our family and friends. The family tradition over the years has been you taking kids to college in your van, and now you're taking your grandchildren, and what a blessing it has been! I thank God for you every single day! We are grateful that he has allowed you to be with all of us and for you to be here to enjoy time with your GREAT GRANDCHILDREN!

You've fought for our country and fought just as hard for people that weren't being treated fairly, whether it was helping a homeless veteran, advocating for a veteran to receive their benefits or speaking up for guys on your job that were afraid to speak up for themselves, you've been a mouth-piece to so many.

When I was younger, you helped me on my first job at Astro World. They told me to clean the bathroom. I inherited your strong work ethic, but I was like, "Oh no, that's for the park maintenance, I'm not cleaning the bathroom. I'm calling MY DADDY!" When my manager got off the phone with you, he told me to just go make the biscuits. LOL

Thank you for your presence, not just your presents. Always know that not only I, but many others, appreciate you as a father, role model, friend and an advocate for those that were afraid. Your strength, resilience, kindness, and love has been exemplified throughout your life. I love you and I'm grateful to call you the world's hero, My Daddy! Thank you for being our rock, our inspiration, and our guiding light.

Love you more,

THE ONE AND ONLY

TANYA 💚

LETTER FROM FORMER PRESIDENT BARACK OBAMA

COMMEMORATION OF THE 50th ANNIVERSARY OF THE VIETNAM WAR

BY THE PRESIDENT OF THE UNITED STATES OF AMERICA

A PROCLAMATION

As we observe the 50th anniversary of the Vietnam War, we reflect with solemn reverence upon the valor of a generation that served with honor. We pay tribute to the more than 3 million servicemen and women who left their families to serve bravely, a world away from everything they knew and everyone they loved. From Ia Drang to Khe Sanh, from Hue to Saigon and countless villages in between, they pushed through jungles and rice paddies, heat and monsoon, fighting heroically to protect the ideals we hold dear as Americans. Through more than a decade of combat, over air, land, and sea, these proud Americans upheld the highest traditions of our Armed Forces.

As a grateful Nation, we honor more than 58,000 patriots—their names etched in black granite—who sacrificed all they had and all they would ever know. We draw inspiration from the heroes who suffered unspeakably as prisoners of war, yet who returned home with their heads held high. We pledge to keep faith with those who were wounded and still carry the scars of war, seen and unseen. With more than 1,600 of our service members still among the missing, we pledge as a Nation to do everything in our power to bring these patriots home. In the reflection of The Wall, we see the military family members and veterans who carry a pain that may never fade. May they find peace in knowing their loved ones endure, not only in medals and memories, but in the hearts of all Americans, who are forever grateful for their service, valor, and sacrifice.

In recognition of a chapter in our Nation's history that must never be forgotten, let us renew our sacred commitment to those who answered our country's call in Vietnam and those who awaited their safe return. Beginning on Memorial Day 2012, the Federal Government will partner with local governments, private organizations, and communities across America to participate in the Commemoration of the 50th Anniversary of the Vietnam War—a 13-year program to honor and give thanks to a generation of proud Americans who saw our country through one of the most challenging missions we have ever faced. While no words will ever be fully worthy of their service, nor any honor truly befitting their sacrifice, let us remember that it is never too late to pay tribute to the men and women who answered the call of duty with courage and valor. Let us renew our commitment to the fullest possible accounting for those who have not returned.

Throughout this Commemoration, let us strive to live up to their example by showing our Vietnam veterans, their families, and all who have served the fullest respect and support of a grateful Nation.

NOW, THEREFORE, I, BARACK OBAMA, President of the United States of America, by virtue of the authority vested in me by the Constitution and the laws of the United States, do hereby proclaim May 28, 2012, through November 11, 2025, as the Commemoration of the 50th Anniversary of the Vietnam War. I call upon Federal, State, and local officials to honor our Vietnam veterans, our fallen, our wounded, those unaccounted for, our former prisoners of war, their families, and all who served with appropriate programs, ceremonies, and activities.

IN WITNESS WHEREOF, I have hereunto set my hand this twenty-fifth day of May, in the year of our Lord two thousand twelve, and of the Independence of the United States of America the two hundred and thirty-sixth.

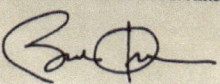

YELLOW ROSE

Why Didn't You Tell Us

Why didn't you tell us about Emily West, who was the "Yellow Rose of Texas"
And some of the rest
I found lots of my people as I started to look
That was part of Texas history, just not in the books
Peter Allen, Henry Arnold, and Joe Travis too
All died for Texas, to just name a few
And the first person on the Texas side to be shot
Was Samuel McCullough Jr., I guess you forgot
And old "Dick the Drummer" left the Mexicans stunned
And confused Santa Anna with the beat of his drums
Now Mr. William Goynes, with all of that land
And businesses, and money, a wealthy black man
There wasn't enough room for our stories to be told
Our value meant nothing, until we were sold
So as for our children they don't have a clue
That the heroes of Texas were black people too
But let us not cry for the ones that are gone
Let's do A little research and write a book of our own
And teach to our children who are with us today
That the future is for everyone and the role they must play
Then we'll all walk together and work as a team
With equality a reality, not one persons dream

Written By: Paul Washington

IN MEMORY OF

<u>Mom</u>
Mollie Washington

<u>Dad</u>
Jim Floyd Washington

<u>Play Grandmother (Baby)</u>
Plesana Leonard

<u>Brothers</u>
Donald Washington
Leon Washington
Floyd Washington
Zachary Washington

ABOUT THE AUTHOR

Mr. Paul Washington was born in Houston, Texas but raised in Crockett, Texas by his Uncle Ben and Aunt Willie Jones and later returned to Houston with his parents Jim and Mollie Washington. He has been happily married to his wife Karen Washington for thirty-three years. Mr. Washington is the father of five adult children, Tanya Rawlins, Michael and Averill Washington (Mother: Irene); Jason and Quincy Thibodeaux (Mother: Jo Ann); Godson Fredinand Durisseau; Step-daughter Nyishia Dillard; thirteen grandchildren and two great-grandchildren.

Mr. Washington is a seventy-five-year-old Vietnam Veteran that served on the frontline in the United States Army from 1969-1971. He retired as an 18-wheeler truck driver after thirty-eight years. For his military bravery, he received seven medals, but his most accomplished medal was the CIB (Combat Infantry Badge) and bronze star. In his leisure time, Mr. Washington loves to read his Bible, spend time with his family and friends, ride his bike in his neighborhood, travel, participate in veteran events throughout the United States and research Texas black history. Mr. Paul Washington is a member of Bread of Life Baptist Church in Humble, Texas under the leadership of Pastor Reginald M. Harris. He became an ordained deacon in 2003 and is currently the Sunday School Superintendent.

Mr. Washington joined the Vietnam Veterans of America, San Jacinto Chapter 343 and have been a life member since 1995. He is a delegate and (MAC) Minority Affair Chair for the Texas State/National Council, where he also serves as the Chaplain of Chapter 343, and member of the African American Library - Gregory Friends, Inc. Mr. Washington's favorite scripture is Psalm 23, "The Lord is my shepherd; I shall not want. He maketh me to lie down in green pastures, he leadeth me beside the still waters. He restored my soul; he leadeth me in the paths of righteousness for his name's sake. Yea, though I walk through the valley of the shadow of death. I will fear no evil, for thou art with me; thy rod and thy staff they comfort me. Thou preparest a table before me in the presence of mine enemies, thou anointest my head with oil; my cup runneth over. Surely goodiness and mercy shall follow me all the days of my life, and I will dwell in the house of the Lord forever."

PHOTO COLLAGE

Throughout the years, Mr. Paul Washington has made a positive impact on the lives of others. Here's a photo collage of him, his family, friends and dignitaries in the community such as: Houston Mayor John Whitmire, Former Houston Mayor Sylvester Turner, and the late, great Congresswoman Sheila Jackson Lee, who has honored him and many other veterans for their courage, strength and dedication. Mr. Paul Washington, a frontline Vietnam War Veteran has left a remarkable legacy that will be unforgettable.

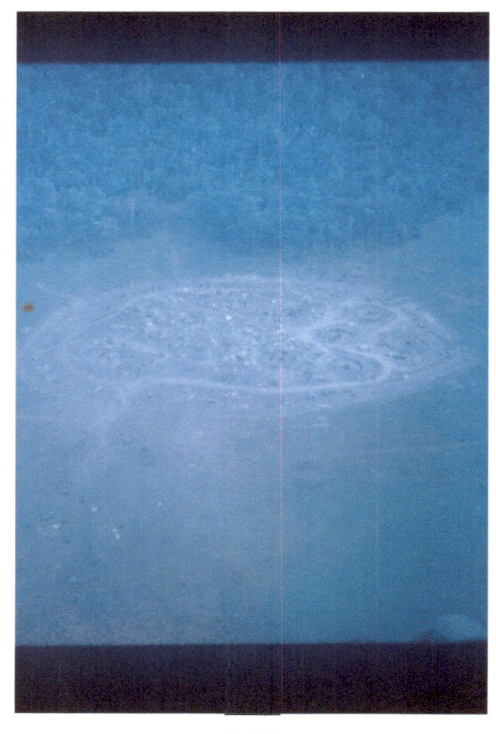

Paul Washington
US Army
Family Friend of
Nylah & Nalin Burrell

BOOKS OF THE BIBLE

27 BOOKS
THE NEW TESTAMENT

4 GOSPELS

Matthew	Luke
Mark	John

BOOK OF HISTORY
Acts

THE PAULINE EPISTLES

Romans	1st Thessalonians
1st Corinthians	2nd Thessalonians
2nd Corinthians	1st Timothy
Galatians	2nd Timothy
Ephesians	Titus
Philippians	Philemon
Colossians	Hebrews

GENERAL EPISTLES

James	1st John
1st Peter	2nd John
2nd Peter	3rd John

Jude

BOOK OF PROPHECY
Revelation

39 BOOKS
THE OLD TESTAMENT

5 LAW BOOKS

Genesis — Leviticus
Exodus — Numbers
Deuteronomy

12 HISTORICAL BOOKS

Joshua — Judges
Ruth — Ezra
1st Samuel — 2nd Samuel
1st Kings — 2nd Kings
1st Chronicles — 2nd Chronicles
Nehemiah — Esther

5 BOOKS OF POETRY

Job — Psalms
Proverbs — Ecclesiastes
Song of Solomon

5 MAJOR PROPHETS

Isaiah — Ezekiel
Jeremiah — Daniel
Lamentations

12 MINOR PROPHETS

Hosea — Joel
Amos — Obadiah
Jonah — Micah
Nahum — Habukkuk
Zephaniah — Haggai
Zechariah — Malachi

"To all the brave men and women who have served our country, we owe you an immense debt of gratitude. Your heroic service, unwavering dedication, and profound sacrifice have shaped the freedoms we hold dear. You have stood at the frontlines, not for recognition, but for the ideals that bind us together as a nation. For every sacrifice, every challenge faced, and every battle fought, we are eternally grateful. Your courage inspires us all, and your legacy will never be forgotten. Thank you and God bless."

For more information about disability benefits, pension benefits, mental health assistance, health care benefits, education benefits, employment benefits, home loan benefits, life insurance, burial benefits and more, contact these Veteran services:

VA benefits hotline: 1-800-827-1000

Veterans Crisis Hotline: 1-800-273-8255

VA health benefits hotline: 1-877-222-8387

GI Bill hotline: 1-888-442-4551

National Call Center for Homeless Veterans: 1-877-424-3838

VA Inspector General: 1-800-488-8244

My HealtheVet help desk: 1-877-327-0022

U.S. Department of Veteran Affairs: 1-800-698-2411

SUSU Entertainment LLC
P.O. Box 1621
Cypress, Texas 77410
www.susuentertainmentllc@gmail.com
www.susuentertainmentllc.com

www.ingramcontent.com/pod-product-compliance
Lightning Source LLC
Chambersburg PA
CBHW042040050526
44107CB00114B/1279/J